BIRDS
OF SOUTHERN AFRICA

Daphne Carew / ABPL

BIRDS

OF SOUTHERN AFRICA

P.A.R. HOCKEY

STRUIK

Front cover: (Main photograph) Malachite Kingfisher (Nigel Dennis/ABPL), (Insets, left to right) African Jacana (Nigel Dennis/ABPL), Crimsonbreasted Shrike (Clem Haagner/ABPL), African Fish Eagle (Nigel Dennis/ABPL).

Struik Publishers (Pty) Ltd
(a member of The Struik Publishing Group (Pty) Ltd)
Cornelis Struik House
80 McKenzie Street
Cape Town
8001

Reg. No.: 54/00965/07

First published 1991
Second edition 1994

Edited by Tessa Kennedy, Cape Town
Design by Joan Sutton, Cape Town
Typesetting by Suzanne Fortescue, Struik DTP, Cape Town

Reproduction by Unifoto (Pty) Ltd, Cape Town
Printed and bound by Kyodo Printing Co (Singapore) Pte Ltd

ISBN 1 86825 517 4

FRONTISPIECE *The Pygmy Falcon is the smallest falcon in the region, weighing a mere 60 grams. Its distribution is intimately tied to that of the Sociable Weaver: it lays its eggs in one of the chambers of the weavers' huge colonial nests.*

PREVIOUS PAGE *The Rufousnaped Lark is a normally inconspicuous species of grasslands and savannas but, during the breeding season, the males sing either in an aerial display or from conspicuous perches such as the tops of bushes.*
Eric Reisinger / ABPL

OPPOSITE *The largest and most powerful eagle of the region, the Martial Eagle, is capable of killing prey up to the size of a small antelope. Although Martial Eagles usually nest in large trees, many nests, especially in the Karoo, are situated on electricity pylons.*
Daphne Carew / ABPL

SOUTHERN AFRICAN BIRDLIFE

Anthony Bannister / ABPL

ABOVE *The Ostrich (female shown) is the largest bird in the world. Although its head is small, it has the largest eyes of any land animal.*

Southern Africa is usually defined as Africa south of a line between the Kunene and Zambezi rivers. The region thus encompasses Namibia, Botswana, South Africa, Lesotho, Swaziland, Zimbabwe and southern and central Mozambique, a land area of approximately 3,5 million square kilometres. Although this represents less than three per cent of the world's land area, more than 10 per cent of the world's birds have been recorded in the region. More than 900 species of birds occur in southern Africa, and more than 700 of these breed in the region. To place this in an international perspective, the whole of North America and Canada, an area six and a half times the size of southern Africa, supports only about 650 breeding species. The bird list for the whole of Australia is only fractionally more than 750 species – compare this with the more than 500 species that have been recorded in South Africa's Kruger National Park alone.

There are some parts of the world which have an even higher diversity of birds: about 1 300 species occur in Venezuela, and Colombia boasts an impressive list of 1 700 species. However, the diversity in southern Africa is sufficiently high, and the birds sufficiently accessible, to have prompted a group of local birdwatchers to make an attempt on the world record for the number of bird species seen in 24 hours.

A high diversity of birds is always exciting to any birdwatcher or nature lover, but there is an added excitement in seeing birds which occur in a restricted area and nowhere else in the world. A bird which occurs only in a particular region or country is described as 'endemic' to that area. Typically, and because they have been isolated for long periods of evolutionary history, islands have high proportions of endemic species. For example, of the bird species which occur regularly in Australia, approximately half occur nowhere else in the world. Smaller proportions of endemic species can be expected in sub-sections of continents, whether they are divided into individual countries or groups of countries. Southern Africa is, however, an exception to this general rule. Of the more than 900 species which have been recorded, 166 (18,5 per cent) are endemic, or nearly endemic, to the region. This makes the area of particular interest not only to birdwatchers, but also to scientists.

There are two main reasons why the diversity of birds in southern Africa is so high – the region's geographical position and its impressive variety of habitats. In all parts of the world, the diversity of birds increases as one approaches the tropics; relatively few species have adapted to life in the cold, high-latitude regions of the world. There are, however, many species which occur in the cool temperate regions and do not extend their distributions into the tropics. Southern Africa straddles the Tropic of Capricorn, and the bird fauna thus has both tropical and temperate elements, ranging from penguins in the south to truly tropical species in the north.

The diversity of habitats in southern Africa is remarkable, and is rivalled by few other places in the world. Landscapes range from the almost waterless deserts of the west coast, to the mistbelt forests of the eastern escarpment, the high montane grasslands of Lesotho and Natal and the woodlands of the north and east. These different habitats all support their own special birds.

Making their living from the abundant food in the cold Benguela Current are a myriad seabirds. The hundreds of thousands of albatrosses, shearwaters, petrels and others which patrol these waters in the search for fish, squid and crustaceans form one of the richest aggregations of seabirds to be found anywhere in the world. Most of these birds do not breed in southern Africa, but visit our waters from their breeding sites at islands in both southern and northern waters, coming from as far away as South America, Australia and Canada. It is likely that their numbers have increased over the past few decades with the advent and development of a large demersal fishing industry. Many of the fish caught in these deep-water trawl nets are not considered of any commercial value and are discarded overboard, providing the birds with a source of food which otherwise would not be available to them.

Some of the seabirds reaping these pastures of plenty do breed locally. A visit to one of the islands off the Cape or Namibian coast is an experience not to be forgotten; tens of thousands of gannets, cormorants and penguins jostle noisily for space in the breeding colonies. Access to most of these islands is difficult and a permit is required. However, Bird Island at Lambert's Bay in the Western Cape has been joined to the mainland by a harbour breakwater and visitors can enjoy the experience of standing among thriving colonies of gannets and cormorants.

In the warmer waters to the south and east of the region there is no major demersal fishery and bird life is less plentiful. Even so, those prepared to venture out to sea for a day from Durban to visit the small prawn-trawling banks are likely to see plenty of seabirds, including shearwaters and albatrosses. Nine of the world's 14 species of albatross have been recorded in southern African waters, but only three of these, the Blackbrowed, Yellownosed and Shy Albatrosses, can be considered common. It seems that the smallest of these, the Yellownosed Albatross, may be unable to compete for food with the larger species on the Benguela trawling grounds. During the winter months, when albatrosses arrive from their southern breeding grounds, Yellownosed Albatrosses are scarce in the Benguela Current area but are common farther north and east. Competition is apparently reduced during the summer months when most adult albatrosses return south to breed; many young Yellownosed Albatrosses move into the Benguela area at this time of year.

In addition to being the most important area for seabirds, the western and south-western coasts also support large numbers of shorebirds such as gulls, plovers and sandpipers. During the summer months, the mudflats of the Berg River estuary in the south-western Cape support the highest density of migratory shorebirds recorded anywhere on the eastern Atlantic seaboard. Although many shorebirds favour estuaries and coastal lagoons such as those at Walvis Bay and Langebaan, large numbers are also found on the open coastline. To a large extent these high numbers are due to the presence of offshore kelp beds. During stormy conditions, which occur regularly – especially in winter – kelp plants are torn from the seabed and washed ashore, sometimes in great mounds. This driftline kelp wrack is colonized by millions of small shrimps, and by the larvae of kelp flies. These small invertebrates provide a rich source of food for the many different bird species which may be seen picking their way among the kelp fronds.

The land adjacent to the west coast provides a stark contrast to the wealth

Anthony Bannister / ABPL

Anthony Bannister / ABPL

TOP *The Yellownosed Albatross is a fairly common visitor to offshore waters from its sub-Antarctic breeding grounds.*

ABOVE *The White Pelican is the larger of the two pelican species occurring in southern Africa; the males may weigh as much as 15 kilograms.*

RIGHT *This African Black Oystercatcher has been marked with a combination of coloured plastic leg rings for individual identification by scientists. Although these birds are locally common, the world population comprises only about 5 000 birds and is entirely restricted to the coast of southern African.*

Anthony Bannister / ABPL

of life on the shore and in the sea. As one moves north from Cape Town along the west coast, the countryside becomes drier and drier until one eventually reaches the seemingly lifeless wastes of the great Namib Desert. Even here, however, there are some species of bird which have become specialized for life in one of Africa's most formidable landscapes. Among the sparse vegetation along a dry watercourse you may see a small bird with a plain brown back that blends superbly with the desert sands. Early in the morning the males sing in a high aerial display. This is the Dune Lark, only recently described to science, and found solely in the Namib Desert. On a visit to see the prehistoric welwitschia plants to the east of Swakopmund one might be lucky enough to see the small and very pale Gray's Lark, another species endemic to the Namib.

Not all birds which occur in the Namib are endemic to this particular desert. Some of them, such as Ludwig's Bustard and the Namaqua Dove, only appear sporadically, usually after one of the rare rain events when the desert is transformed. Grasses suddenly sprout over previously bare dunes, small and brightly-coloured flowers appear seemingly from nowhere, and the insects, reptiles and birds capitalize on this temporary bonanza. Unlike lizards or snakes, the ability to fly allows birds the option of leaving desert areas when the feeding conditions deteriorate. Many arid-country species are nomadic, moving around over a large area in search of sites where rain has recently fallen, food is temporarily abundant, and there is therefore the opportunity to breed. It is usually easy to identify such areas and it is these patches that will prove the most rewarding for the desert birdwatcher.

Moving inland away from the Namaqualand and Namib coasts and on to the great escarpment, aridity still remains the order of the day. The seemingly endless plains of the semi-desert Karoo occupy much of the Cape Province, while to the north lie the red sand dunes of the Kalahari Desert. Although arid, these regions receive on average more rainfall than the coastal lowlands, and this can be seen both in a more complicated vegetation structure and a correspondingly higher diversity of birds. These two areas, along with the adjacent coastal regions, form the south-west arid zone of Africa. Of the 166 bird species endemic to southern Africa, more than 100 have their distribution centred in this arid zone. For example, there are 25 species of larks in southern Africa, 19 of which occur in the south-west arid zone. Of these 19, 13 are endemic to southern Africa and nine of these are essentially endemic to the arid zone. The biology of many of these desert species is not well known. The nests and eggs of two endemic lark species, Sclater's Lark and the Red Lark, were only discovered and described for the first time in the 1980s. During a recent research expedition, three experienced field ornithologists saw four canaries which they could not identify near Verneukpan in the central Karoo. Despite the fact that two of these birds were adult males, the ornithologists were unable to reconcile them with any species of canary found anywhere in Africa. Perhaps a new species awaits discovery and description!

At first glance, many of the birds in the Karoo appear to be either small and brown or small and grey. These are mostly larks and chats, of which several species are common and widespread in the area. Not all the birds are quite this small, however. In the early morning you may hear a series of short, trumpet-like blasts; this is the far-carrying duet of the Karoo Korhaan, a small endemic bustard. Small parties of the much larger Ludwig's Bustard can also be seen, and, occasionally, you may catch sight of Africa's heaviest flying bird, the Kori Bustard, striding though the veld in the heat of the day in search of insects and lizards.

The Karoo of today is very different to the Karoo of the recent historical past. Two hundred years ago, vast herds of game wandered the plains, but these have long since been hunted to extinction. Small numbers are gradually being reintroduced, but the fencing of farm boundaries will largely prevent the migratory and nomadic movements that these animals undertook prior to the arrival of European settlers. Birds associated with these game herds, particularly the big birds of prey such as vultures, have also largely gone. In many cases these were helped on their way to local extinction by persecution from farmers who considered them a threat to livestock. Some illegal poisoning of birds of prey still takes place in the Karoo, but the general level of conservation awareness is improving and we can only hope that some of the species lost from the Karoo in the recent past will gradually return. More positively, in some parts of the country, vultures are being encouraged to return by the provision of supplementary food for them at 'vulture restaurants'.

To the north of the Karoo lies the red Kalahari Desert. The southern fringes of the desert have been impacted by agriculture, but to the north, in the Kalahari Gemsbok National Park and the great game reserves of Botswana, are found some of the most unspoilt wilderness areas of southern Africa. Game is abundant; the big cats – lion, leopard and cheetah are common, and the birdlife is in a near-pristine condition. In contrast to the Karoo, diurnal birds of prey and owls are numerous and a wide range of species is represented. At one end of the scale are the huge Lappetfaced, Whiteheaded and Whitebacked Vultures, and at the other end, the diminutive Pygmy Falcon – Africa's smallest bird of prey – can be seen perched on open vantage points. In the giant acacia trees which line the riverbeds, massive colonies of Sociable Weavers can be found. It is in these huge colonial nests that the Pygmy Falcons also breed. One of the most characteristic desert raptors is the Pale Chanting Goshawk. This bird, with its long red legs, can be seen perched conspicuously on small bushes and trees. Sometimes they follow honey badgers, feasting on the invertebrates and rodents disturbed by the badgers' diggings.

Desert birds typically are well camouflaged, but there are some exceptions. A harsh scolding chatter coming from the middle of an acacia bush may reveal the presence of a startling red, white and black bird – the Crimsonbreasted Shrike. This shrike has three close relatives in southern Africa, the Southern, Tropical and Swamp Boubous. These three species, however, are predominantly black and white. The bright signal breast of the Crimsonbreasted Shrike could be ascribed to 'aposematic' coloration, that is, a warning to potential predators that the flesh tastes unpleasant. However, the remains of Crimsonbreasted Shrikes have been found at Bateleur nests in the Kalahari, suggesting that at least one species of raptor has chosen to ignore the warning!

Some desert animals have evolved the ability to survive without drinking water, including some desert birds which obtain the water they need from their seed and insect foods. Many other species have to drink, and the presence of waterholes is critical to their day-to-day survival. Artificial

Clem Haagner / ABPL

ABOVE *The Crowned Plover is widespread and common in southern Africa. It has adapted well to urban environments and breeds readily in areas of short grass such as playing fields and parks.*

waterholes have been provided in the Kalahari Gemsbok National Park. Large numbers of doves can be seen around these waterholes at any time of the day and occasional flocks of Namaqua and Burchell's Sandgrouse come down to drink. While watching these birds drinking, one may notice that they are extremely nervous. This is because raptors, particularly Lanner Falcons and Gabar Goshawks, hunt regularly at these waterholes, where prey are concentrated. Gabar Goshawks in particular can often be seen sitting motionless in a dense tree adjacent to a waterhole, waiting for that dove that is less watchful than the others.

Joan Ryder / ABPL

ABOVE *Sandgrouse are characteristic birds of desert and semi-desert environments. The beautiful Burchell's Sandgrouse is common on the red sands of the Kalahari desert and, in the middle of the morning, small flocks may be seen coming to drink at waterholes.*

Surprisingly, in the northern Kalahari Desert lies one of Africa's greatest wetlands, the Okavango Delta. The Okavango River is the largest river in Africa that does not flow into the sea. Instead, it spreads out into a 1 600 square kilometre mosaic of islands, papyrus beds and open waters. Birdlife abounds in this desert oasis. The mornings are pierced by the screams of African Fish Eagles and at night the huge Pel's Fishing Owl perches on boughs over the water from where it drops on to its large fish prey. For the birdwatcher, one of the specialities of the swamps is the Slaty Egret. This bird has a very limited world distribution, extending from the Okavango Swamps north to the Bangweulu Swamps in Zambia. Although it was described to science in 1895 on the basis of three specimens collected at Potchefstroom (where it no longer occurs), little is known of its natural history. Only one small breeding colony, in Botswana, has ever been found.

Although the delta itself lies entirely within Botswana, the Okavango River flows through part of Namibia *en route* from its source on the Benguela Plateau in the Angolan highlands. Namibia is a dry country and water is being abstracted from the Okavango River to be channelled south towards the population centres. It is important to monitor whether this removal of water is having any negative effects on the delta. It would be an unspeakable crime against future generations if a natural heritage as pristine and unique as the Okavango Delta were to be damaged; especially if that damage could have been avoided.

To the north and east of the Kalahari and Karoo lie the grasslands, woodlands and forests of southern Africa. These vegetation types are found in areas where the annual rainfall exceeds 500 millimetres, and they support many species of birds which are absent from the dry west. Most of the grasslands are found at high altitudes, for example in the Drakensberg mountain range. Although there is not a large diversity of birds in these grasslands, a substantial proportion of the species which do occur there are very special indeed, being endemic species with small ranges. The beautiful Yellowbreasted Pipit occurs only in the high grasslands of South Africa and Lesotho. Even more restricted in range are Rudd's and Botha's Larks, both of which have their distribution largely confined to particular grassland types in the southern Transvaal. Except during the summer breeding season, when the males display over their territories, these birds are quiet, inconspicuous and difficult to find. In the high reaches of the Drakensberg, the magnificent Bearded Vulture or Lammergeier can be seen soaring effortlessly along mountain ridges. This species has a feeding technique which is unique among African vultures. Whereas all other vultures tear at the meat and entrails of carcasses, the Bearded Vulture feeds mainly on bones, from which it extracts the marrow. Being weak-billed, it cannot break open the bones by force; instead, it flies upwards with the bones in its talons and drops them on to exposed sheets of rock called anvils or ossuaries. The broken bones are then swallowed, sometimes in quite large pieces. In the same rocky, high-altitude habitat as the Bearded Vulture can be found two species of birds which occur only in the Drakensberg mountains – the Drakensberg or Orangebreasted Rockjumper and the Drakensberg Siskin. Although both species are locally common, their very restricted range makes them highly prized by birdwatchers. Less common, and also restricted to high mountains, is the Mountain Pipit. The existence of this species in southern Africa was only recently recognized. It is present in the mountains only during the summer months; during the winter it is thought, but not proven, to migrate northwards to Angola, Zaïre and Zambia.

The habitats which contain the greatest diversity of birds are the woodlands (savannas) and the forests. These habitats are structurally complex, and several different types of woodland and forest are recognized by botanists. The complex structure of these habitats provides many different niches which are used by different species of birds. An early morning walk in a southern African woodland is an unforgettable experience for the birdwatcher. Small birds abound – flycatchers, shrikes, barbets, warblers, weavers, cisticolas and honeyguides. Some of Africa's most beautiful birds are found here – the rollers, orioles, kingfishers and bee-eaters. Lilacbreasted Rollers are common, and no-one can fail to be impressed by the electric coloration on the upper-wings as one swoops down from its perch on to an unsuspecting lizard or insect. Early in the morning the bush is alive with calls and songs. The characteristic 'kwehh' of the Grey Lourie or 'Go-away Bird' can be heard all around, mingling with the harsh 'kwok kwok kwok' of the Yellowbilled Hornbill and the thin piping whistle of the Grey Hornbill.

The high diversity and abundance of birds and other animals in the woodlands make them a prime hunting site for birds of prey. Many species of eagles, goshawks and others thrive in the woodlands. Goshawks flying bullet-like from one tree to another are often difficult to identify, but slowly soaring eagles or vultures allow for better views and a better chance of identification. Several species of owl frequent the woodlands. Perhaps the commonest is the tiny Pearlspotted Owl, with the false eyes on the back of its head. The bird calls with a loud series of whistles, first ascending and then descending, and can often be heard during the day. It is an inveterate robber of nests and predator of chicks and, as a consequence, is often mobbed by small birds. A wide variety of birds mob these owls, including several species of warblers, such as Icterine and Garden Warblers, which do not breed in southern Africa at all. These warblers breed in Europe and the Soviet Union during the northern summer and migrate south to Africa to avoid the cold of the northern winter.

During the breeding season, most birds build nests, lay eggs, incubate them until they hatch and then feed their chicks until the chicks attain independence. Some species, however, have evolved a way to 'cheat' on this strategy. Known as brood parasites, these birds lay their eggs in the nests of other (host) species. The parasite usually lays only one egg per host nest but, because the parasite doesn't have to rear its own chick, it can lay many eggs during a single breeding season. Four groups of parasites are well represented in the woodlands. Cuckoos parasitize a wide range of hosts from babblers to sunbirds, widowfinches parasitize firefinches, and whydahs parasitize finches and waxbills. The larger honeyguides parasitize mainly barbets and woodpeckers, but the small Sharpbilled and Slenderbilled Honeyguides select smaller hosts such as warblers and white-eyes.

Birdwatching in the woodlands is exciting and rewarding, but perhaps less challenging than birdwatching in the forests. Here, sound becomes as (or more) important than sight in locating the birds. Although many forest birds such as robins and bush shrikes are brightly coloured, they are extremely secretive and inconspicuous. Even when they can be located by their song or call, they can still be a real challenge to see. One of the most secretive of all forest birds is the Buffspotted Flufftail. This tiny crake-like bird creeps around in the leaf litter where its quiet rustling could be mistaken for a mouse or a snake moving through the leaves. Its call is a ghost-like, ventriloquial hooting, usually heard at night or on misty or rainy days. These birds sometimes move into well-wooded urban areas and their eerie hooting has prompted many a nervous person into believing that there are ghosts about!

Anthony Bannister / ABPL

Anthony Bannister / ABPL

TOP *The Narina Trogon, with its stunning plumage of red and iridescent green, is a shy and inconspicuous species of the forest canopy. Its soft, hooting call is usually the first clue to its presence.*

ABOVE *Visitors to the Kruger National Park will find that Greater Blue-eared Starlings are common and tame in several of the camps. They are very similar in appearance to the equally common Glossy Starling and the two species are easily mistaken. While the plumage differences between the two species are slight, the birds have very different calls.*

Forests are found over a range of altitudes in southern Africa, and some forest birds, for example the Orange Thrush, Narina Trogon and Barratt's Warbler, undertake seasonal migrations between high- and low-altitude forests, breeding during the summer in the high-altitude forests and moving into the warmer coastal forests during the winter months.

In keeping with the worldwide trend of bird diversity becoming greater as one approaches the tropics, the number of bird species in southern African forests increases from south to north and also from highland to lowland forests. Fortunately, forests in South Africa are generally well conserved. Farther north, in the eastern lowlands of Zimbabwe, the situation is not so healthy. Slash-and-burn agriculture has taken its toll in places such as the Haroni-Lusitu confluence, an area of high bird diversity, but apparently of little conservation concern.

Unlike the south-west arid zone which is separated from similar habitat elsewhere in Africa by vast expanses of woodland and other mesic habitats, the southern African forests form a continuum with forests to the north. For this reason, there are rather few species which are endemic to southern African forests. At present, there are only 12 true forest species which do not occur outside the region. However, this number may be increased when new scientific techniques, such as the analysis of gene structure, are applied in understanding differences and similarities between species.

Nigel Dennis / ABPL

ABOVE *There are only two species of sugarbird in the world, and both are endemic to southern Africa. The Cape Sugarbird, seen here, occurs in the fynbos of the south-western Cape. Gurney's Sugarbird, a slightly smaller species, is found in the Drakensberg and Soutpansberg mountains and along the Transvaal and Zimbabwean escarpments. The distribution of both species is closely tied to the distribution of proteas.*

It would be wrong to create the impression that the entire southern African landscape is covered in pristine, bird-rich habitats. As elsewhere in Africa, the population of southern Africa is burgeoning and this is placing ever-increasing demands on the natural resources of the region. Overgrazing and associated erosion is a widespread problem in several habitats, including the Karoo and the Kalahari. Over time this leads to the loss of surface soils and seed reserves, and the swelling human population is forced to increase the grazing pressure of livestock on the less eroded areas. Much indigenous vegetation has been lost through the planting of crops, especially wheat, maize and sugar cane. Grasslands are under threat from commercial afforestation, wetlands from drainage and ploughing, and river systems from poor farming practices in the catchment areas. For example, the Tugela River catchment area, an important water supply for both the Transvaal and Natal, has lost more than 90 per cent of its wetlands. Alien plants, both terrestrial and aquatic, have invaded many parts of southern Africa. Many of the introductions were deliberate and made at a time when their consequences were not foreseen. Nowadays, a fortune is poured annually into controlling these aliens, some of which are spread by birds which eat their fruits. Atmospheric pollution and acid rain, until recently considered as primarily First World problems, are causing severe damage near major industrialized centres in the Transvaal.

Despite all these problems, however, southern Africa retains a rich natural heritage: the Etosha and Kruger National Parks, the Okavango Delta, Victoria Falls and the Kalahari and Namib deserts all are places that are known worldwide. In South Africa alone, there are more than 575 nature reserves whose ownership and management is vested in a statutory authority, and nearly every bird species which breeds in South Africa breeds in at least one of these reserves. In a recently compiled Red Data Book for the region (which assesses the conservation status of birds), not one bird species endemic to southern Africa was considered to be endangered or vulnerable. Comforting as that statistic may appear, it cannot be considered an excuse for complacency. We have more than a regional responsibility for ensuring the continued conservation of both the landscapes and the rich birdlife of southern Africa. Many of the birds found here breed elsewhere, but rely on southern African waters, estuaries, woodlands and other habitats to ensure that they survive the period between breeding attempts. There is little point in conserving the breeding grounds of a species if the areas where that

ABOVE *Map of southern Africa showing the major habitat types.*

species spends the non-breeding season are lost. What we have, we have in trust – we must be able to account for it to future generations.

Birdwatchers visiting the region will be pleasantly surprised by the accessibility of the prime birdwatching sites. The road system is excellent, parks and reserves are well organized and there are many good field guides available, both for the whole region and for different subregions. In a three-to-four week visit, a keen birdwatcher should be able to see between 500 and 600 species of birds. The greatest diversity of birds can be seen during the summer months (November to March), when the local bird fauna is supplemented by migrants from the northern hemisphere. Seabirds, however, are at their most plentiful during the winter months (July and August).

At whatever time of year you choose to visit the region, however, you can be assured of a wealth of birdwatching excitement and wonder – a single African Fish Eagle yodelling close to your camp in the early morning with the mist rising off the river, or a flight of salmon-pink flamingos at dusk are images and memories that can never be erased. The early morning rush of bird activity on a warm lowveld morning or the sight of hundreds of vultures spiralling high above you are experiences as African as the trumpeting of an elephant or the roaring of a lion. The fascinating diversity of plant and animal life found in southern Africa cannot be viewed in isolation from the rest of the 'dark continent'; it is part of Africa's heritage. Absorb it, enjoy it, but don't damage it.

Johan van Jaarsveld / ABPL

LEFT *The Dabchick has a very wide distribution in the Old World and occurs throughout Africa, south of the Sahara. It builds a floating nest and, after the young hatch, they often ride on the parents' backs.*

BELOW *The Jackass Penguin, named because of its donkey-like braying call, is endemic to southern Africa, breeding on the offshore islands and at one or two sites on the mainland. The population is very much smaller than it was 100 years ago, due largely to egg collecting and disturbance to its breeding habitat caused by guano collecting.*

OVERLEAF *The Cape Gannet occurs only in southern Africa, and the entire world population breeds at only five colonies, four on the west coast and one on the south coast. The population is increasing and other colonies may form in the future.*

Anthony Bannister / ABPL

Anthony Bannister / ABPL

Nigel Dennis / ABPL

ABOVE *The stiletto-like bill of the Darter is used to spear its fish prey underwater. Its habit of swimming very low in the water, with only the head and neck visible, has earned this species the alternative name of 'snakebird'.*

RIGHT *The Cape Cormorant is far and away the most abundant cormorant of the region. It characteristically fishes and roosts in large flocks which may sometimes comprise more than 100 000 birds. This species also breeds in large colonies, but in many years the breeding success is very low and large numbers of chicks apparently starve to death.*

Anthony Bannister / ABPL

Reg Gush / ABPL

Nigel Dennis / ABPL

Nigel Dennis / ABPL

Clem Haagner / ABPL

OPPOSITE *The Goliath Heron is a huge tropical species, standing nearly a metre and a half tall. It stands motionless in the water for long periods, waiting to spear a large and unsuspecting fish.*

TOP *The Grey Heron is a common and widespread species throughout much of the Old World.*

LEFT *The Cattle Egret is a highly adaptable and successful species frequently associated with man and his livestock.*

ABOVE *As its name suggests, the Blackcrowned Night Heron is almost exclusively a nocturnal hunter.*

BELOW *Long legs, a striking black and white plumage and multi-coloured bill ensure that the Saddlebilled Stork cannot be mistaken for any other bird in the region. This is a tropical African species which extends its distribution in southern Africa only as far south as Zululand.*

RIGHT ABOVE *The Black Stork is a northern hemisphere species which has a small, isolated breeding population in southern Africa. There are similar isolated breeding populations of White Storks, Booted Eagles and European Bee eaters.*

RIGHT BELOW *During the summer months, tens of thousands of White Storks visit southern Africa from their breeding grounds in the northern hemisphere. These birds are potentially of great benefit to farmers as much of their diet consists of locusts and other large insects.*

Gavin Thomson / ABPL

Anthony Bannister / ABPL

Nigel Dennis / ABPL

Anthony Bannister / ABPL

Anthony Bannister / ABPL

ABOVE LEFT *The long, slightly decurved yellow bill and the red facial skin distinguish the Yellowbilled Stork from other storks of the region. These birds are almost invariably associated with water, and feed together in small groups. Within the region, they breed regularly only in Botswana and Zimbabwe.*

ABOVE *Marabou Storks are huge birds, with a heavy, strong bill and bare, pink skin on the head and neck. They eat a wide range of prey, much of which is scavenged: they are gregarious birds and can often be seen clustered around carcasses feeding together with vultures and crows.*

ABOVE *The far-carrying 'hadeda' call of the Hadeda Ibis is one of the most characteristic sounds of the moister eastern parts of the region. In recent years, due in part to the artificial irrigation of farmlands, this species has rapidly expanded its range westwards along the south coast and has now colonized the Cape Peninsula.*

RIGHT *The Hamerkop is a bird shrouded in African myth and superstition. Although not a particularly big bird, it builds an enormous, domed nest in the fork of a large tree. These nests are sometimes taken over by other species: Giant Eagle Owls have been known to chase Hamerkops away from the nest, and empty nests are regularly used by Egyptian Geese.*

Anthony Bannister / ABPL

Nigel Dennis / ABPL

Nigel Dennis / ABPL

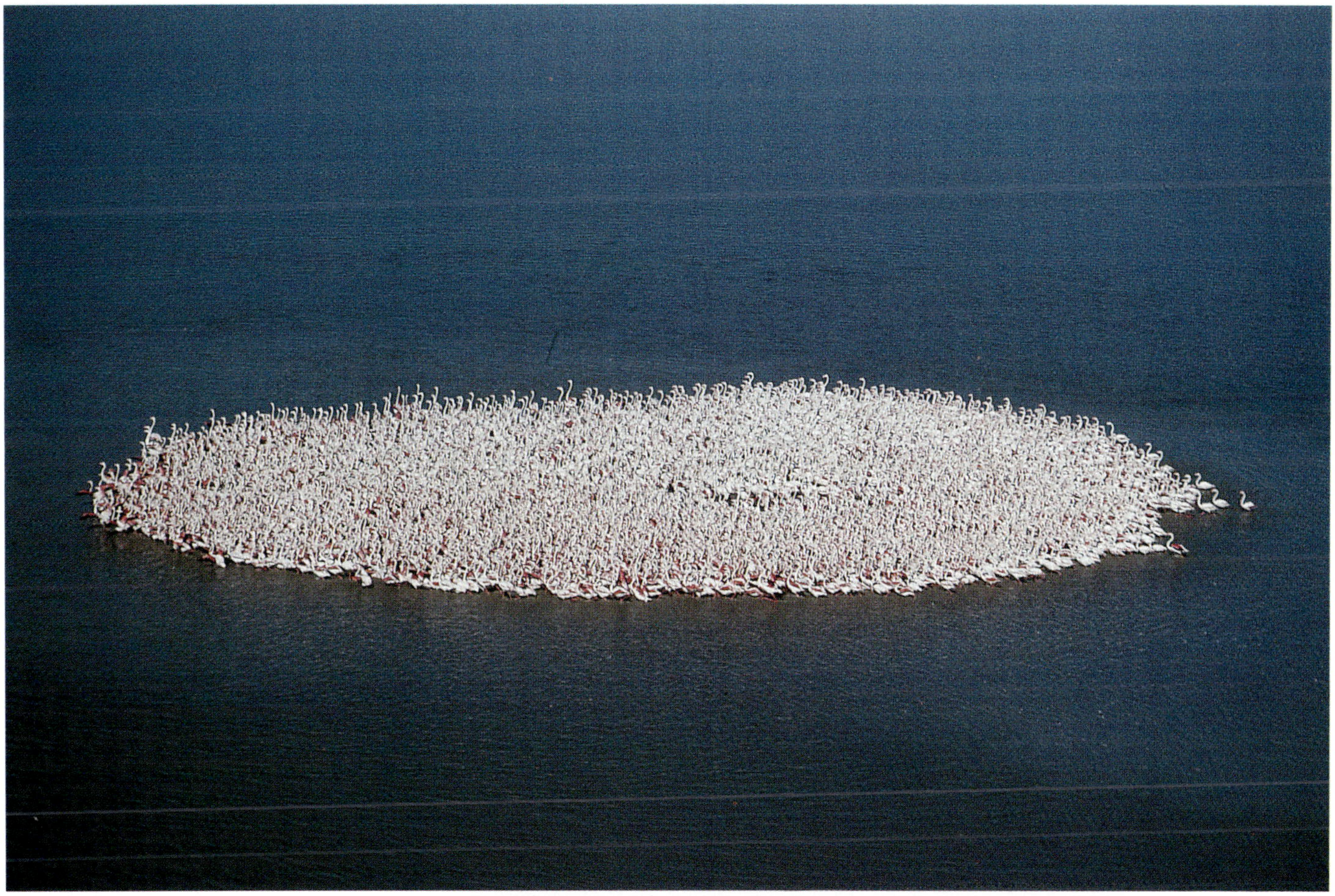

Tim Liversedge / ABPL

LEFT *The spatulate bill of the African Spoonbill gives the bird its name. While feeding, the African Spoonbill sweeps its slightly open bill from side to side in the water, sifting out small fish and invertebrates such as shrimps.*

ABOVE *This large flock of Greater Flamingos was photographed at the Sua Pan in Botswana. Although Greater Flamingos can be seen at many waterbodies throughout the region, they only breed at large ephemeral inland waterbodies such as Etosha Pan and the Makgadikgadi Pans. Breeding attempts at other sites almost invariably fail.*

RIGHT *In contrast to the Greater Flamingo, which feeds mainly on small crustaceans, the much smaller Lesser Flamingo is a specialist feeder on blue-green algae which it sifts from the water column. It is able to do this by means of hair-like structures in the bill which are analogous to the baleen of the large filter-feeding whales.*

Anthony Bannister / ABPL

Joan Ryder / ABPL

LEFT *One of the most widespread waterfowl in southern Africa is the Egyptian Goose. Correctly a duck, not a goose, this species can be found from the largest lakes to the smallest of farm ponds, even in the most arid habitats. It adapts well to urban areas and occasionally hybridizes with domestic ducks.*

BELOW *The Yellowbilled Duck is one of the most common ducks in southern Africa. During the non-breeding season it gathers in large flocks, sometimes feeding on agricultural lands. In urban areas it may hybridize with introduced Mallard, a species to which it is very closely related.*

RIGHT *The Fulvous Duck is found in the tropics of both the Old and New Worlds. It is one of two species of 'whistling ducks' found in the region, the other being the Whitefaced Duck.*

Nigel Dennis / ABPL

Terry Carew / ABPL

OVERLEAF *The Spurwinged Goose is the largest of the region's waterfowl, with the males weighing as much as 10 kilograms. Although it is not common in the arid west, elsewhere it occurs in large numbers. When not breeding it gathers in large flocks, which sometimes feed in croplands where they cause some damage.*

Nigel Dennis / ABPL

Clem Haagner / ABPL

LEFT *The very long legs and strange head plumes of the Secretarybird make it one of the most unusual-looking birds of prey in the world. In addition to appearing bizarre, it has an unusual hunting technique whereby it stamps on its prey, which range in size from insects to fairly large snakes.*

BELOW *The Cape Vulture is endemic to southern Africa, and the present population is much lower in number than it was historically. The reasons for this decrease include a shortage of food as a result of the loss of the great herds of migratory mammals and gradual improvements in stock-farming practices. Further losses occur through direct persecution even though the species is fully protected by law.*

Reg Gush / ABPL

BELOW *The Bearded Vulture must rank as one of the most beautiful of Africa's raptors. Even though it is a large vulture, it is not strong or aggressive enough to compete with other vultures for food at carcasses. Instead, it feeds largely on the bones left behind when the stronger scavengers have had their fill. Using an unusual feeding strategy, it takes the bones in its talons, flies up and then drops the bones on to hard surfaces called anvils or ossuaries. It then picks up the broken bones and swallows them.*

Nigel Dennis / ABPL

Lorna Stanton / ABPL

Nigel Dennis / ABPL

Lorna Stanton / ABPL

LEFT *In flight silhouette, the Crowned Eagle appears more like a huge hawk than an eagle. Crowned Eagles are confined largely to dense forests where they are able to fly agilely between the trees. They are extremely strong and take large prey such as monkeys and antelopes.*

ABOVE LEFT *Superficially resembling the slightly smaller Peregrine Falcon, the Lanner Falcon can be identified by its rufous hind-crown. The Peregrine Falcon's hind-crown is black.*

ABOVE RIGHT *As its name suggests, the Blackbreasted Snake Eagle is a specialist hunter of snakes. Although the bird itself weighs on average only one and a half kilograms, it is capable of catching and subduing snakes of up to two metres long.*

Anthony Bannister / ABPL

Anthony Bannister / ABPL

The power and grace of an African Fish Eagle as it swoops on to a large fish is surely one of Africa's unforgettable sights. The sight and sound of this bird will be among the strongest memories that any visitor to the large rivers and dams of southern Africa will take home.

ABOVE *This adult Jackal Buzzard illustrates perfectly the poise and accuracy that a raptor needs to make a successful strike at its prey.*

RIGHT ABOVE *The Pale Chanting Goshawk is one of the most conspicuous raptors of the arid west and is often seen scanning the ground below for prey from the high vantage point of a telegraph pole. In the Kalahari, Pale Chanting Goshawks have been found to hunt in association with honey badgers, searching for small mammals and insects disturbed by the badgers' digging.*

RIGHT BELOW *The Greater Kestrel is primarily a bird of the arid regions. Rather than build its own nest, it usually takes over the abandoned nests of other raptors or crows. In much of the Karoo, most of these nests are placed on electricity pylons rather than in natural vegetation.*

Anthony Bannister / ABPL

Nigel Dennis / ABPL

Er c Reisinger / ABPL

Anthony Bannister / ABPL

Clem Haagner / ABPL

RIGHT *The Blue Crane is South Africa's national bird. Apart from a small and geographically isolated population centred on the Etosha National Park, the entire population is confined to South Africa and Lesotho. The largest aggregations occur in the wheatfields of the southern Cape.*

Reg Gush / ABPL

Daphne Carew / ABPL

ABOVE *The range and numbers of Wattled Cranes in southern Africa have been severely reduced in the past 150 years, and the species is now considered endangered in South Africa. The main reasons for the decrease are disturbance, poisoning, trapping and loss of breeding habitat.*

OPPOSITE *The striking plumage and elaborate dancing displays of the Crowned Crane are fortunately still common sights in the south-east and north of southern Africa. Like the Hamerkop, this species figures prominently in African folklore and it is not disturbed or persecuted in rural areas. There are, however, still occasional mass mortalities when these attractive birds eat poisoned grain.*

Lisa Trocchi / ABPL

Nigel Dennis / ABPL

Nigel Dennis / ABPL

LEFT *The male Blackbellied Korhaan is well known for his spectacular aerial display in which he tumbles towards the ground, apparently out of control, opening his wings only just before he reaches the ground.*

ABOVE *The Kori Bustard is Africa's heaviest flying bird: the male may weigh as much as 19 kilograms. The huge wings required to lift this weight off the ground give the in-flight Kori Bustard the appearance of a flying carpet rather than a bird.*

Nigel Dennis / ABPL

Eric Reisinger / ABPL

ABOVE *The African Finfoot is a reclusive bird of quiet tropical rivers and streams. The first clue to its presence is often a splash as the bird drops off a branch or bank into the water and swims away, largely submerged.*

LEFT *The Purple Gallinule is a large brightly coloured resident of well-vegetated waterbodies, where it feeds mainly on the underground parts of water plants such as rushes and sedges. These it pulls up with its bill and then holds in one foot while it eats them.*

Lorna Stanton / ABPL

LEFT *The Threebanded Plover is a resident species which lays its eggs in a shallow scrape on the ground close to water. Because such a nest is potentially at risk from predators such as mongooses, the eggs are very cryptically coloured and difficult to see against the background of the nest lining, which often comprises small sticks.*

BELOW *The extremely long toes of the African Jacana allow it to balance as it walks across floating vegetation. This behaviour has earned it the alternative name of 'lilytrotter'.*

Nigel Dennis / ABPL

RIGHT *Most resident waders in southern Africa lay smaller clutches of eggs than their counterparts in Europe, but may lay several clutches during a year. The Avocet is an exception and usually lays four eggs, the same as in Europe. The reason for this is probably the choice of nesting site. Avocets usually breed at ephemeral waterbodies and thus have a limited time available for breeding.*

Terry Carew / ABPL

RIGHT *The Redwinged Pratincole is an uncommon summer visitor to the region. It is a wader, but its very short legs, long wings and forked tail give this bird a swallow-like appearance. The pratincoles are the only waders which hunt on the wing, feeding on aerial insects.*

BELOW *Although dikkops are largely nocturnal, they can often be seen during the day roosting quietly in the shade of a bush or tree. The Water Dikkop is one of two species of dikkop in southern Africa and can be recognized by the pale grey and white bars on the folded wing.*

OPPOSITE *Temminck's Courser is unusual in that its favoured feeding sites are disturbed areas such as heavily grazed pastures, recently burned veld and ploughed fields. These habitats tend to be short-lived and consequently the birds are nomadic, moving regularly between different areas.* Clem Haagner / ABPL

Tim Liversedge / ABPL

Daphne Carew / ABPL

Anthony Bannister / ABPL

ABOVE LEFT *The Grey Loerie is also known as the 'Go-away Bird'. Its 'go-away' or 'kwee' call is one of the most familiar sounds of the bushveld and can be heard at any time of the day.*

ABOVE *Rosyfaced Lovebirds are popular cage birds, but their natural habitats are the deserts and desert fringes of the dry west. They nest in a variety of sites including, as illustrated here, the chambers of Sociable Weavers' nests.*

Lorna Stanton / ABPL

Lorna Stanton / ABPL

LEFT *The tiny Pearlspotted Owl is a common resident of the northern bushveld and savanna regions. It is active and calls during the day, when it is frequently mobbed by small birds. It has the unusual plumage feature of a pair of false 'eyes' on the back of its head.*

ABOVE *The Wood Owl is a characteristic bird of the eastern and northern lowland forests. Pairs have an evocative and far-carrying vocal duet which can be heard during spring and early summer when they are breeding.*

Tim Liversedge / ABPL

ABOVE *Visitors to the Okavango Swamps or the larger rivers of the eastern lowveld may catch a glimpse of the magnificent Pel's Fishing Owl. This species roosts during the day, emerging at night to hunt for fish from low overhanging branches.*

RIGHT *The sharp-eyed visitor to the Kalahari Gemsbok National Park will almost certainly see Giant Eagle Owls roosting in acacia trees along the roadside. The birds are very approachable and their huge size, soft grey plumage and conspicuous pink eyelids make this species unmistakable.* Lorna Stanton / ABPL

Lorna Stanton / ABPL

Anthony Bannister / ABPL

LEFT *The Cape Eagle Owl is an uncommon species of rocky and mountainous areas. Although it is sometimes confused with the Spotted Eagle Owl, it is a much larger bird with noticeably more powerful feet and talons. This difference in size is reflected in the prey taken by the two species; whereas the Spotted Eagle Owl eats mainly small rodents and large insects, the Cape Eagle Owl preys mainly on mammals the size of hares and dassies.*

ABOVE *The Spotted Eagle Owl is common throughout most of southern Africa. It may be seen perched on roadside poles in the late afternoon and early evening, waiting to pounce on unsuspecting rodents. Its habit of hunting along road verges means that this species is often killed by cars at night.*

Tim Liversedge / ABPL

OPPOSITE *The electric coloration of the Malachite Kingfisher can be remarkably cryptic when the bird is perched among dead reeds. This is a common species of vleis, marshes and rivers throughout the region and is the smallest of the fish-eating kingfishers.* Tim Liversedge / ABPL

LEFT *The loud, trilling call of the Woodland Kingfisher is a common sound in the northern and eastern woodlands. Although it is a kingfisher, this species eats mainly insects and reptiles, and very rarely catches fish.*

BELOW *The breast of the female Giant Kingfisher (shown here) is white with black spots, whereas that of the male is chestnut. The Giant Kingfisher and the Pied Kingfisher are the only kingfishers of the region which regularly forage along the open seashore, usually in rocky areas.*

Anthony Bannister / ABPL

Joan Ryder / ABPL

Anthony Bannister / ABPL

ABOVE LEFT *The Swallowtailed Bee-eater, seen here perched at the entrance to its nesting burrow, is one of nine species of bee-eaters that have been recorded in the region. It has a stronger preference for desert and semi-desert areas than any of the other local bee-eaters.*

LEFT *The startling reddish-pink and turquoise coloration of the Carmine Bee-eater makes it impossible to confuse with any other species. This bee-eater breeds in large colonies in river banks, migrating north to equatorial Africa after breeding.*

Anthony Bannister / ABPL

Tim Liversedge / ABPL

ABOVE *Some species of bee-eaters roost in tightly packed lines on branches. This behaviour, seen here in Little Bee-eaters, probably serves to conserve heat and may provide an efficient early warning system for detecting a potential predator.*

LEFT *The Hoopoe occurs in a wide range of habitats, including urban areas where it probes in lawns for insects. The long, black-tipped crest is fanned when the bird is alarmed.*

Clem Haagner / ABPL

Gavin Thomson / ABPL

Rob Ponte / ABPL

Tim Liversedge / ABPL

OPPOSITE ABOVE *The Redbilled Hornbill is a common resident of the northern savannas, occurring in small flocks throughout most of the year. Apart from the bill colour, this species is similar in overall appearance to the Yellowbilled Hornbill, but is smaller.*

OPPOSITE BELOW *The Yellowbilled Hornbill is a common resident of bushveld and savanna. In many of the picnic sites and rest camps of nature reserves and national parks this species has become tame and confiding.*

ABOVE *Although the Ground Hornbill is by far the largest hornbill in southern Africa, it retains the smaller hornbills' habit of nesting in holes in trees. Unlike the smaller hornbills, however, the female is not sealed into the nest chamber. Ground hornbills live in groups: only one female in the group lays eggs and when she is incubating she is fed by other members of the flock.*

LEFT *Hornbills nest in natural cavities in trees. All the incubating is done by the female, who is sealed into the cavity and fed by the male. After the young hatch, the female breaks the seal and emerges. The young hornbills partially reseal the entrance, after which they are fed by both parents. Here a Yellowbilled Hornbill is seen at the entrance to the nest cavity.*

Clem Haagner / ABPL

Clem Haagner / ABPL

LEFT ABOVE *The noisy duet of a pair of Blackcollared Barbets is a common sound in the suburban fringes of many towns and cities in the east and north of the region. Unlike the hornbills, these birds excavate their own nest chamber in a tree trunk or branch.*

LEFT BELOW *One way of getting around the problem of raising your own young is to lay your eggs in the nest of another species and let the other parents do the work. Here a Forktailed Drongo feeds a young African Cuckoo which is already larger than its host parent.*

RIGHT *The Blackheaded Oriole is common and widespread in forests and woodlands in the higher rainfall areas of the region. The male (shown here) is brightly coloured but its habit of perching in the very tops of tall trees renders it more often heard than seen.*

Anthony Bannister / ABPL

Joan Ryder / ABPL

ABOVE *The nest of the Paradise Flycatcher is a delicate structure of lichen, bark and small plant fragments bound together with spiders' web. The male, seen here, has a spectacular long chestnut tail; that of the female is shorter.*

RIGHT *The Longtailed Shrike is a striking and common resident of bushveld and savanna. It is a co-operatively breeding species, which means the breeding pair is assisted in raising the chicks by one or two other birds. These 'helpers' are likely to be related to the breeding pair.* Clem Haagner / ABPL

Anthony Bannister / ABPL

ABOVE *The Puffback gets its name from a highly conspicuous display given by the male during courtship. The long white rump plumes are erected and puffed up over the back to look like a large cotton ball.*

Anthony Bannister / ABPL

LEFT *The Bokmakierie is the most common shrike of the arid western regions. It is highly vocal, particularly in the early morning, and both members of the pair almost invariably sing in duet. Although the duets comprise a large repertoire, one of the most frequently given calls is a 'bokmakierie', from which the bird derives its name.*

BELOW *The tiny Collared Sunbird is a fairly common resident of evergreen forest and coastal thicket in the south and east of the region. It is one of the few sunbirds in which the male and female plumages do not differ substantially.*

Johan van Jaarsveld / ABPL

Johan van Jaarsveld / ABPL

Anthony Bannister / ABPL

Clem Haagner / ABPL

OPPOSITE *The heavy bill of the Bully Canary allows it to eat seeds and fruits which are too large or hard for smaller-billed canaries to handle.*

ABOVE *The Cape Weaver is endemic to South Africa and Lesotho. Within its limited range it is common, breeding in colonies either in reedbeds or in trees, often overhanging water.*

LEFT *Male Masked Weavers build several nests within a colony and may mate with several different females. If a nest is not accepted by a female, it is usually destroyed by the male. Masked Weavers are common throughout the region, occurring in a very wide range of habitats.*

ABOVE *The diminutive Blue Waxbill is common in bushy habitats throughout the east and north of the region. This species is usually seen in small flocks which drink regularly at water points.*